20 GREAT
CAREER-BUILDING ACTIVITIES USING
INSTAGRAM®
AND SNAPCHAT®

EDUARDO LOPEZ

ROSEN
PUBLISHING®

New York

Published in 2017 by The Rosen Publishing Group, Inc.
29 East 21st Street, New York, NY 10010

Copyright © 2017 by The Rosen Publishing Group, Inc.

First Edition

Library of Congress Cataloging-in-Publication Data

Names: Lopez, Eduardo, 1989– author.
Title: 20 great career-building activities using Instagram and Snapchat / Eduardo Lopez.
Other titles: Twenty great career-building activities using Instagram and Snapchat
Description: First Edition. | New York : Rosen Publishing, 2017. | Series: Social media career building | Includes bibliographical references and index.
Identifiers: LCCN 2016021379 | ISBN 9781508172727 (library bound)
Subjects: LCSH: Instagram (Firm)—Juvenile literature. | Snapchat (Electronic resource)—Juvenile literature. | Business networks—Juvenile literature. | Employment portfolios—Juvenile literature. | Career development—Juvenile literature.
Classification: LCC HM743.S53 L67 2017 | DDC 650.1/3—dc23
LC record available at https://lccn.loc.gov/2016021379

Manufactured in China

References to and uses of Instagram and Snapchat do not imply endorsement or sponsorship, and our publication is for informational purposes only relative to possible uses of the Instagram and Snapchat sites.

CONTENTS

INTRODUCTION

We are a deeply visual species. As the internet has grown around us, we use it to tell stories about ourselves. We once could form bonds only in person, but the internet changed everything. It gave us an infinite number of possibilities to modify the world we live in. Programmers gave life to online chat rooms and social networks that helped people connect, belong, and feel free to be themselves, creating a new kind of community. We now form deep meaningful relationships with people all over the world using the internet.

Billions of people around the world can now broadcast images and videos every hour through social media networks. Instagram and Snapchat users across the globe are relaying information that can help a student learn a new language, get hired for a dream job, or get accepted into a reputable university.

The emergence of social media has helped visual content become one of the most powerful ways for people to build a reputation for their talents. This resource will teach you how to use Instagram and Snapchat to build a portfolio that you can use to impress potential employers or schools. Show the world you have what it takes to make a difference!

The best way to tell a story is visually. Images and videos can relay so much complex information in a much quicker period. This helps you digest more information in a faster way!

CHAPTER ONE

How Visual Content Became King

Before Instagram and Snapchat, there was the blogging platform LiveJournal. In 1999, the "social web" was just becoming popular and the internet was much simpler. Web videos were small and slow, so text was king of content. Text-based networks like chat rooms and LiveJournal were the dominant "social media" platforms of the time. These were the first tools that allowed users to keep in touch online.

Recently, the world has shifted more to applications that mimic qualities of physical connection—two-way video calling, audio messages, and animated GIF images. Visual content is now the most popular medium produced by companies and media outlets.

HOW DID INSTAGRAM BEGIN?

Kevin Systrom, the founder of Instagram, graduated from Stanford University, interned at Twitter, and worked

Video humanizes written communication. Today, it is estimated that three out of every five people are using their smartphones or mobile devices for video calling.

at Google before founding Instagram in March 2010 at age twenty-eight. In 2009, Systrom spent his days as a product manager for Nextstop.com, a travel start-up that Facebook acquired in September 2010. At night, he poured his time into learning code.

Systrom left his job in March 2010 to build an app called Burbn, hiring his first employee, Mike Krieger, a twenty-five-year-old engineer. They grew unhappy with Burbn, so they decided to cut everything in the app except for its photo, comment, and like capabilities.

After three years of massive success, Instagram CEO Kevin Systrom gave 130 million people access to video. This announcement finally made it possible for users to shoot video with multiple cuts and filters.

The cofounders settled on the name Instagram and went live in October 2010. At the end of the first week, Instagram had been downloaded one hundred thousand times. By December, the community had grown to a million users. Instagram now has a community of more than four hundred million users, making it larger than Twitter!

HOW DID SNAPCHAT BEGIN?

In 2008, Snapchat founder Evan Spiegel joined the Kappa Sigma fraternity at Stanford, where he met

Bobby Murphy, Snapchat cofounder and the programmer behind the app. In 2009, Spiegel and Murphy tried launching their first app, Future Freshman LLC, but it failed to garner any attention. In April 2011, Spiegel and Murphy were about to complete their junior year at Stanford when their friend Reggie Brown had an idea: "I wish these photos I am sending this girl would disappear."

By the summer, the idea of Snapchat was born. The team spent the summer working on the app, with Spiegel as chief executive officer, or CEO, Murphy as chief technology officer, or CTO, and Reggie Brown as chief marketing officer, or CMO. In August, an argument occurred between Brown and Spiegel over the order of names on the technology patent and the distribution of

Snapchat creators Spiegel and Murphy didn't succed on their first try. Their 2010 launch of Future Freshman, which helped teens, parents, and counselors deal with the college admissions process, failed.

PROMOTING YOUR LIFESTYLE TO CREATE BONDS WITH YOUR AUDIENCE

Alex Hayes, a seventeen-year-old from Australia uses Instagram to document his adventures and travels. With more than sixty-eight thousand followers, he uses his account to promote brands that feature people living healthy lifestyles. Brands started hearing about Hayes after he won a few semiprofessional surfing competitions, launching him into Instagram popularity. Shortly after, he created a convincing Photoshop hoax that appeared to show the surfer with a shark lurking under his board.

In 2014, Nutri-Grain paid Hayes $5,000 to for forty posts promoting their #FuelOn hashtag. Nowadays, Hayes considers a successful Instagram post one attracting at least three thousand likes.

company equity. Brown left the company. Renamed Snapchat, the service relaunched in fall 2011. A few months later, the company had grown to one hundred thousand users.

In 2013, Spiegel was being criticized by many for turning down a $3 billion cash acquisition offer from Facebook. Today, the company is valued at more than $19 billion and has more than one hundred million daily active users.

CHAPTER TWO

Getting Started on Instagram

Whether this is your first time setting up an Instagram account or you are already using it to keep in touch with your friends, the following section will help you build a themed portfolio that attracts followers from the ground up.

SETTING UP YOUR ACCOUNT

An Instagram portfolio is incredibly easy to get started. Although Instagram offers a desktop version of the app, where you can view your profile, browse your newsfeed, and view posts, if you want to register for an account you need to download the app directly on your mobile device.

Download the app and sign up with Facebook or your email. Choose a username and password, and you're ready to start building and designing your portfolio. Your profile consists of a profile picture, a short bio (personal description) with a link, and the images you post. You

The easiest way for people to find you online is to use a consistent username across all your social media accounts.

can choose to make your profile private or public, but your profile picture is always public.

When you're first setting up your profile, it's important that your bio and username remain consistent with your other social profiles. For example, if you are thinking of starting a website or you already have one for your portfolio, make sure your username and bio match your website domain and About Me section. This makes it easier for followers to find you across platforms.

Your name and username are also the only fields that Instagram considers in search queries, so make sure your information is consistent across all social networks to help Instagram and search engines make it easier for universities, employers, and potential fans to find you on the Internet. The easier it is to see consistency in your values and focus across platforms, the more you'll connect with followers who want to engage with your content.

Here are some helpful tips to keep in mind when designing your bio:

- Choose a recognizable username.
- Use a logo, a work sample, or a presentable photo of you for your profile picture.

- Include a link to your website, blog, or any other social media channel you want users to connect with (Twitter, Facebook, Tumblr, etc.).

Your bio and website link spaces are great places to get creative with the way you promote yourself. These are the only areas Instagram offers for users to include a clickable link, so take advantage and update it each time you publish a new blog post, promote other social channels, or include details about any upcoming videos, events, or projects.

INSTAGRAM'S BASIC FEATURES

Instagram is a platform centered around building a community and discovering engaging content. On Instagram, users can choose to make their accounts public or private, which controls who can follow them and see the posts to their account. Your account is identified by your username, which allows other people to search for you. You can use your name or just pick a username, also called a handle.

There are many different features available in Instagram's interface. Your bio is the place to share a bit about yourself. When you first open the app, you'll see your feed, which shows other users' uploads. This can be sorted by relevancy or chronological order. You'll see all of the uploads, known as posts, of the users you follow.

When making a photo or video post, users can apply filters to edit the image. Posts include a photo or video along with an optional caption that can include hashtags, a location tag, and sometimes other users tagged by their handles. On each post, other users can like the content and also comment on it. Comments and likes on your posts will appear in your notifications. Another way to see and share posts is through a direct message (DM), which arrives in your in-box.

You'll see posts appear in an Activity Feed, which shows when a user likes or comments on one of your photos, when your photo is posted to a popular page, or when you are tagged in a photo by another user. If you'd like to see more posts from people you don't follow, check the Explore tab, where you can browse content, search for content, and discover featured content. This also contains a search function, where you can search for users based on handle or real name. It also allows you to search for hashtags and locations.

EXPLORING PHOTOS AND VIDEOS

Once your profile is set up, it's time to start exploring around and finding accounts to follow. The more users you follow, the more people will be exposed to your account. Start with your friends. Next, consider which universities, businesses, or experts you want to follow you. Form a relationship with them by consistently commenting on and engaging with their posts.

Use the Explore and Activity tabs to search for users, hashtags, and places. The hashtag section is also a great place to see what keywords are best for your portfolio because you can see how many times users use certain hashtags. When you search for a place or location on Instagram, a map appears showing all the photos that were taken with a location tag, which is also called a geotag. Whenever you add a location to your own photos, a post is uploaded to your photo map.

TAKING, EDITING, AND SHARING PHOTOS

No one will want to follow an empty Instagram profile, so upload a photo or video before you start attracting users to your account. To publish a post, tap on the

A personalized Videos You might Like channel lists videos from across Instagram. As you scroll through the Explore grid, you may also see Featured channels filled with videos on specific topics.

camera icon at the bottom of the screen. Here you can choose to upload a photo or video from your phone's library or capture a new one.

After you've uploaded or taken a new photo or video, you'll have the option to crop it, adjust it, or add filters. If you posted a photo that is square shaped, the app will let you straighten and adjust your image by sliding bars left and right to adjust the degree. You can also rotate a photo by hitting the rotate icon in the upper right corner.

Instagram is known for its filter section, which allows you to add preset effects to your posts. There are now forty filters, but don't worry, you won't need to scroll through all of them each time. You can actually pick which filters you want to see and sort them in the order you want them to appear by using the Manage feature at the end of the filter selection.

Here are some helpful tips to keep in mind when uploading a post:

- Always caption and use a hashtag.
- Use natural lighting during early morning, late afternoon, and overcast days for best quality.
- Use the grid to position your pictures better before capturing them.
- Get closer to what you're trying to capture and record to improve quality.

INSTAGRAM DIRECT

Instagram has a built-in messaging system called Instagram Direct. Its main purpose is to let you send private photos with accompanying text to friends or groups, but you can also use it to send photos you see in your Instagram feed to your friends.

To see messages you've sent with Instagram Direct, tap the button in the top right of your own feed. Posts sent with Instagram Direct can't be shared to other sites like Facebook or Twitter. You're not able to tag people in messages, and messages sent using Instagram Direct won't appear on hashtag and location pages.

FIND YOUR COMMUNITY WITH HASHTAGS

Hashtags are one of the most interactive features of Instagram. Users place these distinct tags into captions and comments to join an existing conversation or create space for like-minded users to discover relevant content. You can create a hashtag out of any phrase by placing a # before a word or phrase. If you want to tap into popular hashtags, you can check out some of these:

#foodporn A widely popular hashtag for photos of delicious meals.

#ootd OOTD stands for "Outfit of the Day." Used to show what you are wearing on Instagram.

#regram A regram is a repost on Instagram. It's similar to a retweet on Twitter and used to give credit to the original poster.

#tbt Hashtag that is short for "Throwback Thursday." Thursdays are when Instagram users share photos from the past.

INSTAGRAM ETIQUETTE

You're less likely to upset—or even alienate—followers and casual viewers if your follow some basic rules of etiquette. If you're using the apps for to promote yourself, your work, or your business, the last thing you want is to drive away potential fans or customers by insulting them! Sticking to a few common-sense safety tips is also a smart move.

Professional photographers say that the best Instagram content is produced when you plan it out ahead of time. First, think about what's in your life and what you want to share with your audience.

GENERAL TIPS

- Do not repost pictures without giving the original poster credit.
- Do not post illegal content, such as photos showing contraband, offensive behavior, or nudity.
- Do not overpost, especially when it comes to selfies, dog photos, and baby pictures.
- Do not purchase followers or likes; this is considered to be abusing Instagram and is looked down upon.

SAFETY TIPS

- Never share your social security number (or the last four digits), birth date, home address, or phone number.
- Don't share posts that disclose sensitive information. For example, do not share an Instagram image of your house and mention that you are home alone in the caption. Be aware of the information you share; others could use for malicious purposes.
- If you find yourself uncomfortable or harassed on Instagram, you can make use of the block and report feature. You can block users, and as well as report their actions.

CHAPTER THREE

Creating a Content Plan

I n this chapter, you'll discover how to find your voice and position yourself online. You will also learn how to create a calendar that lets you organize ideas for pictures and video posts to share, as well as help you visualize how your content will be distributed throughout the year.

Planning, creating, and publishing content can be hard if you aren't organized. Once your calendar is in place and has been in use for a period of time, you'll be able to identify gaps in your content plan and have a bank of content ideas.

 DEFINING YOUR GOALS

Understanding your online identity is an important first step to deciding what content you should be sharing on social media. Answer the questions in the activity below to help inform your social media guidelines and content plan.

What's your overall objective for using Instagram?
What are your goals?
How will you measure your success?
What does your audience want to see?

 ## CREATING YOUR MISSION STATEMENT

A mission statement is a brief sentence explaining your portfolio's purpose and the reason why it exists. The best way to manage your time and resources

Find a focus for your portfolio and determine how it fits into your content strategy. This saves you from either neglecting a profile or automatically posting the same content across all your channels.

JUSTIN BIEBER: DISCOVERED ON SOCIAL MEDIA

At the age of twelve, Justin Bieber was posting videos of himself on YouTube. First his videos only gathered a hundred views, then a thousand, then ten thousand, so he started posting more videos. After a while, some industry insiders like Usher and Justin Timberlake started taking notice.

There was a bidding war between Timberlake and Usher, but Usher eventually won out and Bieber signed to Island Def Jam records.

Today, Justin Bieber is considered an international superstar. He became the first artist to have seven songs from a debut record chart on the Billboard Hot 100 and even had a concert film called *Justin Bieber: Never Say Never* in 2011. The star is now worth more than $200 million, and it all started through social media.

Although this was accomplished through YouTube, you can still use this technique to showcase your talents on Instagram and Snapchat. Are you a great photographer? Share it with the world; you never know if you'll be the next Justin Bieber.

is to find a focus for your portfolio and consistently share videos and photos that support that goal. Defining what you want your account to achieve will also help you focus on the steps you need to take to succeed.

Answer the questions in the following activity to help find your focus and guide your mission statement.

What do you do?
How do you do it?
Who do you do it for?

 ## FINDING YOUR CONTENT THEMES

Identify a few categories or subtopics to add depth to your content. Each category should tie directly back to something you're showcasing in your portfolio.

Demonstrate your talents and qualities with the categories for your Instagram or Snapchat portfolio. If you're looking to get a job out of this project, make sure to share content that highlights your skills, finished projects, trainings, networking events, and other relevant items. If you're looking to get accepted into a school, demonstrate your passions, your beliefs, your academic awards, school events, and all other applicable groups or activities.

 ## CREATING A CONTENT CALENDAR

Decide what you're going to post and when you plan to publish it. Be sure to tie your images and videos to your content themes in the calendar and keep the desired action in mind. If you want someone to message you about job opportunities, make sure your post idea reflects that.

Using a calendar to plan what you post on your account can force you to focus on your long-term goals.

If you don't feel comfortable creating your own calendar, services like Hootsuite offer options for content planning and easy scheduling and sharing. Try visiting the Hootsuite website and downloading Hootlet. Some programs or extensions, like Hootlet, let you add additional apps like Flipboard, Trendspottr, and Content Gems that suggest relevant content for you to share.

 ## TRACKING YOUR SUCCESS

Now that you know what you're going to be posting about, it's important that you stay focused on your goals. The only way to find out if you're building a successful portfolio and producing good content is to keep track of your results. Tracking the engagement—including likes, messages, and shares—can show you what's appealing to your followers and what isn't. Then you can brainstorm ways to adjust your strategy to improve your results.

Come up with a set of ways to measure your content—these measurements are called metrics.

For example, if you want to measure the growth of your followers, your metrics would be the number of adds and follows you receive.

You can track your success with a variety of metrics. Some examples include awareness, engagement, conversion, and advocacy. Make

Tracking followers and engagement is a great way to make your results meaningful, actionable, and targeted.

notes of your objective, the results you are looking for, and the metrics you will use to determine success. You can compare these notes to the actual results afterward to give you concrete information on what to work on in the future as you grow your portfolio.

CHAPTER FOUR

Getting Started on Snapchat

I f you've never used Snapchat or you're interested in starting a new account, the following section will teach you about what is necessary to build a great portfolio on Snapchat. For those of you already using the app, this section will teach you about some best practices and ways to improve your Snapchat.

SETTING UP YOUR ACCOUNT

Creating a Snapchat account can be done in a matter of minutes. The first step is to download the app. Snapchat can only be used on a mobile device. Once you're done installing Snapchat, open the app and click the Sign Up button. Enter your email address, password, and birth date. Then choose your username.

You won't be able to change your username, so try to match it to your other social media accounts. Snapchat is different from social networks like Facebook and Instagram, which suggest accounts to add or follow. This is important to keep in mind when you choose your username because people need to know how to follow your portfolio. Choose a short unique name that's easy to remember and spell.

Unlike Instagram, Snapchat doesn't have a profile or bio section, but it does let you create a custom profile picture called an avatar. Choose between a still image, logo, or animated image by clicking on the ghost icon on your profile page. Either upload a picture or press the button to begin recording a series of shots the app will use to create your animated image.

Once you've picked a username, you will be asked to link your mobile number. This is one way you can let people who have you in their address book find you on Snapchat, but you can skip verifying that if you do not wish to share it. You can also look for other users to follow using the Add Friends option. However you can only search for other users if you know their exact usernames.

Having an account and a profile image is only the first step; you still need to make sure your account is protected. Go to your privacy settings and enable the two-step verification feature that requires a password in addition to a code sent via text in order for someone to log in to your account on a new device.

SNAPCHAT'S BASIC FEATURES

Snapchat is built around units of content called snaps and stories. A snap is an image or video message you send to another user or group of users privately. A story

grantmain
Score: 6

☺ Added Me

Add Friends

Snapchat's ghost logo is named Ghostface Chillah, which is a play on the name of the rapper Ghostface Killah.

is a snap you share with your friends or the public. Your story remains public. You can also send multiple snaps to your story in one day, and they will combine to create one story. In addition to snaps and stories, you can use the chat feature, which allows you to privately message with friends on Snapchat.

When you are connected with a user and you both follow each other, you are each others' friend. If someone follows you who you are not following back, that person is a follower. A follower can view your stories, but you won't be able to send them snaps. Sending and receiving gives you a score on the app, which is the total number of snaps you have sent and received.

EXPLORING SNAPCHAT

Stories are compilations of snaps that create a narrative and honor the true nature of storytelling. Stories appear in chronological order with a beginning, middle, and end. Go to your newsfeed and click Stories to see what users are sharing publicly on Snapchat. Adding a snap to your story allows Snapchatters to view your snap for an unlimited number of times for twenty-four hours.

Here are some tips for navigating around Stories:

- Tap to skip to the next snap in a story.
- Swipe left to skip to the next story.
- Pull down to exit!

PROFITABLE CAREERS VIA SNAPCHAT

Christine Mi always assumed she'd use her economics degree from Yale to go into finance or management consulting, but instead she became a professional Snapchat artist. Mi first started creating complex Snapchat doodles as a way to take breaks from her homework and make her friends laugh. However, things changed for Mi a few months into 2014 after some of the artwork she had been sharing on Tumblr went viral.

An agency reached out and asked if she would be interested in using her skills commercially, working with brands. Years after becoming famous on Snapchat, Mi is still being paid to create unique content for brands and for uncovering new strategies to improve a brand's reputation and increase its profits. Keep this in mind when building your online portfolio—you might not end up where you originally wanted to go, and that's okay. There's more than one way to be successful when you're building an online reputation!

Snapchat overhauled its Lenses animations in late 2015. However, you can still check out old classics, if you like. All you have to do is change the date on your phone to a date from the past!

Featured stories will appear in the Live section of your Stories screen until the event is over.

Story Explorer lets you dive deeper into a moment in a story you liked. If you're attending a concert, just swipe up on a relevant live story to see similar snaps that were also submitted to the topic. To return to the original post, just swipe down or tap the circular icon in the top-right corner of the screen.

There's more to the app than sending pictures. Swipe right on a friend's name in your Snapchat feed to start chatting! If you see a blue dot at the bottom of your chat screen, it means your friend is in the chat.

Chats disappear after viewing, just like a picture or video sent to a specific person.

If your friend is available, he or she also has the option to watch or join a live video session. You will be unable to see friends who choose to watch but they can hear and see you and also send you chats. If they join, you will be able to see and hear each other.

DISCOVER ON SNAPCHAT

Snapchat's Discover feature gives users a series of channels where media outlets can share streams of photos, videos, and articles with users. This feature was solely created for companies and organizations to express their ideas and inform users about topics they are passionate about.

To find Discover, navigate to the Stories screen, and tap a channel icon to dive in. Swipe left on the Camera screen to open the Stories screen. Tap the screen, or swipe left to skip to the next Snap. Swipe up on a Snap you're interested in to learn more. Pull down to exit a channel.

Press and hold on a channel icon for a quick summary of what it has to offer. To see more channels, just swipe on the row of channels in the Discover section, or tap the purple circle in the top-right corner of the Stories screen.

Press and hold on the screen to snap what you're reading or watching to a friend. Or if you want to save a story for later, just tap the down-facing

Following the unwritten code of Snapchat etiquette not only makes your experience safe and productive, but it also makes your content more concise, effective, fun, and engaging for everyone involved.

arrow to save it to your device's photo library. Snapchat has also introduced "memories," an in-app way to save snaps.

ETIQUETTE

Snaps and stories aren't meant to last, but that doesn't mean that ettiquette isn't important on Snapchat. Sticking to the following tips will show that you respect your followers and that you have put some real thought into the snaps and stories you generate.

- Do not double-up, or add a snap you just sent to your friends to your story.
- Avoid unnecessary background noise; mute your image when you have a noisy background.
- Avoid blurry photos and videos.
- Never share your social security number (or the last four digits), birth date, home address, phone number, or the state where you were born.
- Only take appropriate photos and videos. Remember that people can take screenshots!
- Edit your privacy settings so only people you know can engage with you.

CHAPTER FIVE

Creating a Plan for Your Snapchat Content

In this chapter, you'll learn how to position yourself on Snapchat. This will also give you insight into how to tie your goals to a content calendar.

DEFINING WHAT'S IMPORTANT TO YOU

Understanding your online identity is an important first step to deciding what content you should be sharing. Snapchat has its own considerations: content is spontaneous, with fun details like animated filters, text, and stickers. Consider the unique features of Snapchat, and then answer the below questions to inform your personal guidelines and content plan.

What is your goal for Snapchat?
What is the desired action from your audience?
What is the specific type of content the audience wants to get in this channel?
How often will you be posting?

CHOOSING YOUR VOICE AND POSITION

Choose three words that capture the personality of the voice you want for your brand. Then pair each of those three words with a word that limits and clarifies the original word. For example:

- Confident but not arrogant.
- Funny but not offensive.
- Smart but not complex.

To inform your voice, research what other popular users are posting about and discover techniques you may be interested in using. Look at the ways your audience communicates. Are they formal or informal? Detail oriented or focused on big ideas? Are they casual and conversational? Motivate your audience by incorporating action verbs and short phrases to maximize dramatic effect and impact.

CHOOSING YOUR CONTENT THEMES

One of the biggest mistakes social media users make is changing their day-to-day messages. Think about DJ Khaled's recent rise to Snapchat fame. Khaled dominates the entire platform with a series of themed videos, including Fan Luv, Major Key (about the keys to success), We the Best, and Mogul Talk.

DJ Khaled is one of Snapchat's most prolific snappers. By 2016, the number of young people following him was greater than the number watching *The Big Bang Theory*, television's top-rated show.

Offering consistent, identifiable themes through personal behind-the-scenes content is the best way to use and promote yourself on Instagram and Snapchat. When your presence has a pattern, followers will crave your content and expect it.

Create your monthly content calendar for planning out your themed posts in advance. What do you want to be seen as? (Artist, musician, athlete, engineering student, writer, scientist, entrepreneur, etc.) Use your previous answer to pick four categories that support that vision. How often will you post each theme? What day of the week? What time?

 ## TRACKING YOUR SUCCESS

Although we discussed measurement in an earlier chapter, when it comes to Snapchat and its temporary

 ### > TALENT AGENCIES FOR SOCIAL MEDIA CELEBRITIES

Jérôme Jarre became a Snapchat celebrity at the age of twenty-two. He posted his first video on Vine in January 2013 on the day Vine launched. Three months later, he posted a video that became one of the earliest videos to go viral on the platform. Half a year after starting his account, Jarre had gained more than twenty thousand followers.

Jarre considered himself an entrepreneur and started to use his comedic videos as a platform for a future business. His efforts landed him a feature in the popular website BuzzFeed, where one author praised Jarre's Humans project, and noted "this Vine project will restore your faith in humanity."

Jarre now broadcasts comedy to his 1.2 million Snapchat followers and promotes the talent agency he founded for Vine and Snapchat stars called GrapeStory! The agency now has more than thirty Vine stars signed on, among other kinds of social media celebrities.

While Snapchat is looking to build a tool to help users measure their efforts, in the meantime users should focus on measuring engagement, story completion, and follower growth.

posting style, the process may need a little tweaking. Measuring Snapchat can be done a variety of ways, but which method you use highly depends on your preference, how many posts you've published, and what makes the most sense for your own unique goals and vision. Here are some measures of success:

Consistency: Do you frequently and consistently post content?

Relevancy: Does your audience need the content you're providing?

Style: Does your content engage your market?

Efficiency: Do you have an efficient process for selecting/curating content?

Influence: Is your market share improving every month?

Goals: Does your content support your overall goals? Is it working?

Challenge: Are the calls to action that you issue producing results?

CHAPTER SIX

Building Your Portfolio

In this chapter, you'll start to build your portfolio on Instagram and Snapchat. This will help you decide how you will be showcasing your skills on both platforms and also serve as a guide to approaching potential schools, employers, mentors, customers, fans, or experts.

CREATING AN INSTAGRAM PROFILE IMAGE

The profile image or avatar you choose for your Instagram account will shape how your friends, fans, and followers see you. It is the first impression you give to your audience. You may want to select an appropriate professional headshot or photo as a profile picture. If you want to highlight your work as an artist or chef, you could use a photo of a painting or dish you made, instead. Make the most of this opportunity to shape others' mental images of you.

Science says profile pictures are important! One study by Toronto's York University found that humans can draw conclusions about people's photos within as fast as 40 milliseconds!

CREATING A SNAPCHAT PROFILE IMAGE

For your Snapchat profile image, you can take and use a selfie or an animation made up of several selfies. It's very easy to do. Start by clicking on the ghost icon that appears on the top of the screen when you open the app. This will let you access the Snapcode Selfie screen, which looks like an empty, enlarged version of Snapchat's familiar ghost logo. After pressing the

You can use your profile image to add new friends! Friends can point their Snapchat camera at the image and scan it to automatically add you to their friend list.

capture button, your front-facing camera will take a number of burst-shot pictures that the app will use to create the images that will appear inside the ghost.

 # INTERVIEWING EXPERTS

Interviewing experts is a great way to get a reputation as a leader in your area. After you decide who you want to talk to, write an email requesting an interview. Let the person know what you're doing, why you're doing it, and what you want for the interview. Here's a sample to give you some ideas:

> Dear [name],
>
> I'm currently a junior at Barbara Goleman High School and I want to study marketing in college. I created a Snapchat portfolio to showcase my talents and attract potential schools.
>
> Every Tuesday I host "Talent Tuesdays," where I Snapchat a Q&A with an expert in the field. I would love to interview you for an upcoming video on the future of marketing.
>
> An interview would be easy and could be done over Skype. Do you have any availability this week for a short Skype call?
>
> Thank you for your time.
>
> Best,
> [Signature]

Followers will see you as more trustworthy because they will associate you with the expert's reputation. As an added bonus, experts often share interview videos with their networks, so this will help you reach more people and get the word out about your account.

 ## PREPARING FOR INTERVIEWS

Whether you are interviewing an expert or a friend, be prepared. Write a list of five to ten questions to ask in the interview. Here are some examples:

Make sure you plan your interview. Keep it brief and concise, and above all else, be personal and do your homework on the person you're interviewing.

How did you get started in this area?
Can you tell us about the clients you work with?
What are the keys to success?
What sort of obstacles do you deal with?
How do you overcome them?

 ## HOW IT'S DONE/MADE

Think about the skills on your résumé and the ones you want to show off through your Instagram or Snapchat portfolio. Are you a writer? Show samples of how to write a book. Try guiding the audience through a step-by-step tutorial or showing the process through a series of snaps.

Write three ideas for posts or stories you can share on Instagram or Snapchat. One example would be taking five photos (or making five short videos) on how to write a short story. Using a step-by-step format, explain to users how they can:

- Brainstorm an idea.
- Make an outline.
- Write a first draft.
- Edit their story.
- Publish their story.

 ## LIVE EVENT COVERAGE

Attending events is a great way to network and meet potential employers, friends, professors, mentors, investors, and partners. Many reputable events are also an excellent source of continuing education, allowing you to catch up on the latest industry trends, issues, and solutions.

For your audience, sharing videos of these events highlights that you're dedicated to your talent, hobby, or profession and gives you opportunities to network with others and tag them in pictures you took together. Introduce yourself to a person you would like to know and ask if he or she could share a tip or a piece of advice with your social network and request to take a picture. Incorporate your subject's answer into the caption and use the event hashtag. Then, tag the

Whether you're at a small local event, a school-wide event, or a huge conference, social media can be used to amplify the news in a powerful way!

person or send him or her a picture through social network, so your subject has the option to share it with his or her followers as well.

 ## BEHIND-THE-SCENES LIFESTYLE

When people review portfolios, they look to understand the person's personality through several factors, such as their work, writing, education, or interests. Are you an artist? Show them what a day in the life of an artist is like. Let them follow you on the way to class, share your time sketching, get a glimpse of your home life, and so forth.

Think about ways that you could share content on Instagram and Snapchat to show exclusive access to an event or project. Try writing three ideas for posts or stories you can share on Instagram or Snapchat.

For example, if you're working as a volunteer at a sporting event, walk around and ask athletes for interviews. Ask what they think about their challengers and how they're going to prepare for the event. Share these interviews on Instagram or Snapchat with your followers. Be sure to ask the athletes if they can share your posts on social media!

 ## OFFER A SNEAK PEEK

Sneak peek videos are a great way to make your audience feel they are part of an exclusive club with insider access into the production process. They also build support and anticipation around your projects and initiate additional opportunities for two-way conversations with potential employers or schools.

Mexican singer Anahí also used this when she recorded her new music video in 2016. She took pictures and posted several videos on Instagram showing different looks from the set, her doing tons of yoga to prepare for the music video, and intense workouts she was doing to maintain her health.

Write three ideas for posts or stories you can share on Instagram or Snapchat. An example is to share the process of writing your next blog post. Talk about the topic you're going to write about and what drove you to want to discuss it. Talk about why it's important and hint at when you plan to publish the post. Share random quotes from your post that will pique your audience's interest and make them want to read your blog when the post is published.

 ## VISUALIZING A RÉSUMÉ

In 2015, graduate student Elski Felson was on a mission to land a job at Snapchat. Using short video clips, he went line-by-line through what Snapchat was looking for in a candidate and showed humorous reasons why he exemplified those requirements. Felson's videos went viral, even landing him coverage in *USA Today* and BuzzFeed.

Think of creative ways to use your portfolio to make a video. If you have a résumé, go through it line-by-line and visualize it. If you don't, write one up, including all the jobs you've had, volunteer work you've done, and activities you've participated in at school.

Social media is great way to promote your work. Mexican singer Anahí used social media to start a conversation around her new album. This led E! Online to cover her in a feature article.

IDENTIFYING INFLUENCERS

Be sure to follow the accounts of your favorite companies and schools. Identify and follow accounts of people you admire, companies that inspire you, and schools you respect. Make a list of ten accounts to follow that you will later reach out to about your portfolio. Go through these accounts and follow the

Today's job recruiters don't want to know what you can do, they want to see what you've done. Visualized resumes allow you to give employers sample footage of what you have to offer in action.

EXTRA TOOLS FOR INSTAGRAM

There are a variety of apps you can download to get tools to use in Instagram. For example, Layout makes it easy to make collages on Instagram. The Quick app lets you add text to an image. Afterlight is great for photo editing, while Canva is useful for both photo editing and graphic design. You can download the Vintagio app for video editing. The Lapse It app makes it easy to make time-lapse videos. If you're looking to plan out your videos, you might try using the Storyboarder app.

There are also apps that help you schedule your posts if you know you're going to be busy to post or off the grid for a while. The Later app (which was once known as Latergramme) offers an easy way to schedule Instagram posts. If you'll be free to make the posts you've queued up yourself but would like reminders to do so, consider using the TakeOff app.

ones that appear relevant or helpful as examples you can use to learn. They can provide great ideas to help boost your success rate on social media.

 ## WRITING A SCRIPT

Canadian-born American comedian King Bach used scripted comedy skits to become famous on social networking sites like Vine, Twitter, Instagram, and Snapchat, eventually becaming the most-followed person on Vine. His online stardom led to him signing with UTA talent agency and landing roles in *House of Lies* and MTV2's *Wild 'n Out.*

Try writing a script for your videos and reach out to each of the accounts you discovered when identifying influencers on the platform. Come up with creative ways to engage a potential employer or school.

CONCLUSION

Visual content is one of the most influential ways to convey information, and social networks like Instagram and Snapchat allow you to harness its power and use it to elevate your reputation.

Using the lessons you learned in this book, you are now ready to start planning and creating content. You're also ready to engage and promote your portfolio to employers and schools.

Remember to always create and direct images and videos strategically, post consistently, and track your progress along the way. Using these strategies, you'll reach your goal in no time at all!

GLOSSARY

avatar A visual representation of a user online, though not necessarily an actual photo of the user.

bio The area located under your name on your profile that is designated for writing a small description about yourself.

block To prevent another user from following you or viewing your posts.

comment An interaction between users; you must be tagged by your username in order to receive a notification.

direct message A feature that allows you to send and receive private messages.

feed Found under the Home tab, this shows a the images and videos from those you follow. This may be sorted by relevancy or chronological order.

filters Preprogrammed unique photo effects that combine several elements, including exposure, color balance, and contrast.

follower Someone who follows you on social media. They can view your posts and stories.

friend A user you've mutually connected with. On Snapchat, both of you have to have added each other as contacts to become friends.

geotag The location attached to an image, which corresponds to a longitude and latitude on a map. This allows your photos (if public) to be viewed alongside all other photos at this location. In order to display images, you must allow Instagram to access your GPS location.

hashtag Any word or phrase with the symbol # written before it (no spaces). This allows users to connect with others and discover images based on a common word or phrase. The symbol is also called an octothrope or a pound sign.

like A function that means that someone liked your photo or video; done by double-tapping the image itself or by clicking the Like button at the bottom of the image.

metrics A system of standard measurement to track your results.

photo map The world map that displays where your images were geotagged. In order to display images, you must allow Instagram to access your GPS location.

score In Snapchat, the total number of snaps you have sent and received.

snap A video or still image you capture with your device's camera within the app and then send to another user or upload to your Snapchat story.

story A snap you share with your friends or the public. Your story remains public and available to view an unlimited amount of times within twenty-four hours. You can also send multiple snaps to your story in one day, and they will combine to create one story.

username Sometimes referred to as your handle, this is the name of your account; it is one way for users to find you.

FOR MORE INFORMATION

Contently
598 Broadway
New York, NY 10012
(646) 767-6826
Website: http://www.contently.com
Contently is an award-winning technology company
that helps brands create content. They provide
businesses with smart technology, content-creation
advice, and creative talent like journalists, photographers, designers, and videographers.

Content Marketing Institute
17040 Amber Drive
Cleveland, OH 44111
(888) 554-2014
Website: http://www.contentmarketinginstitute.com
The Content Marketing Institute is the leading global
content marketing education and training organization, teaching people and brands how to attract
and keep a following through good storytelling.
They host the largest content marketing–focused
event, called Content Marketing World, every
spring and publish the bimonthly magazine *Chief
Content Officer*.

CoSchedule
503 7th Street N
Fargo, ND 58102
Website: http://www.coschedule.com
CoSchedule is a content marketing company that helps
people and companies plan blogs, social media,
and other content. Today more than ten thousand

content marketers, bloggers, and influencers use CoSchedule's products for their websites and social media accounts.

Hubspot
25 First Street, 2nd Floor
Cambridge, MA 02141
(888) 482-7768
Website: http://www.hubspot.com
Hubspot is an Internet marketing company that sells software designed to attract and engage followers with relevant, helpful, and personalized content and marketing. They help people and brands get more visitors to their website and make more online sales.

Media Smarts
950 Gladstone Avenue, Suite 120
Ottawa, ON K1Y 3E6
Canada
(613) 224-7721
Website: http://www.mediasmarts.ca
Media Smarts is a nonprofit organization that provides digital and media literacy. Its goal is to teach children and teens the critical thinking skills needed to become active and informed digital citizens.

Social Media Examiner
13025 Danielson Street
Poway, CA 92064
Website: http://www.socialmediaexaminer.com
Social Media Examiner is a media company that publishes online magazines, blogs, and podcasts

about how people can use social networks. They help millions of businesses discover how best to use social media to connect with people, drive traffic, generate awareness, and increase sales.

WEBSITES

Because of the changing nature of internet links, Rosen Publishing has developed an online list of websites related to the subject of this book. This site is updated regularly. Please use this link to access the list:

http://www.rosenlinks.com/SMCB/insta

Ascher, Steven. *The Filmmaker's Handbook: A Comprehensive Guide for the Digital Age.* New York, NY: Plume, 2012.

Fromm, Megan. *Ethics and Digital Citizenship* (Media Literacy). New York, NY: Rosen Publishing, 2015.

Gaetan-Beltran, Daniel. *Social Networking* (Issues That Concern You). Farmington Hills, MI: Greenhaven Press, 2015.

Handley, Ann. *Everybody Writes: Your Go-to Guide to Creating Ridiculously Good Content.* Hoboken, NJ: Wiley, 2014.

Kawasaki, Guy. *The Art of Social Media: Power Tips for Power Users.* New York, NY: Penguin Group, 2014.

Miles, Jason G. *Instagram Power: Build Your Brand and Reach More Customers with the Power of Pictures.* New York, NY: McGraw-Hill Education, 2013.

Meyer, Susan. *Understanding Digital Piracy* (Digital and Information Literacy). New York, NY: Rosen Publishing, 2015.

Norris, Dan. *Content Machine: Use Content Marketing to Build a 7-Figure Business with Zero Advertising.* CreateSpace Independent Publishing, 2015.

Pulizzi, Joe. *Content Inc.: How Entrepreneurs Use Content to Build Massive Audiences and Create Radically Successful Businesses.* New York, NY: McGraw-Hill Education, 2015.

Pulizzi, Joe. *Epic Content Marketing: How to Tell a Different Story, Break through the Clutter, and Win More Customers by Marketing Less.* New York, NY: McGraw-Hill Education, 2013.

Robb, Bill. *Snapchat: Complete Guide to Using Your Snapchat to Its Fullest: Tips & Secrets Guidebook.* Amazon Digital Services LLC, 2016.

Safko, Lon. *The Social Media Bible: Tactics, Tools, and Strategies for Business Success.* Hoboken, NJ: John Wiley & Sons, Inc., 2012.

Stockman, Steve. *How to Shoot Video that Doesn't Suck.* New York, NY: Workman Publishing Company, 2011.

Suber, Howard. *The Power of Film.* Studio City, CA: Michael Wiese Productions, 2006.

Vaynerchuk, Gary. *Jab, Jab, Jab, Right Hook: How to Tell Your Story in a Noisy Social World.* New York, NY: HarperBusiness, 2013.

BIBLIOGRAPHY

Bakhshi, Saeideh, David A. Shamma, and Eric Gilbert. "Faces engage us: Photos with faces attract more likes and comments on Instagram." *Proceedings of the SIGCHI Conference on Human Factors in Computing Systems*, pp. 965–974. ACM, 2014.

Caputo, Tony C. *Visual Storytelling: The art and technique.* New York, NY: Watson-Guptill Publications, 2003.

Holt, Douglas. "Branding in the Age of Social Media." *Harvard Business Review*, March 2016 Issue, 40–48, 50.

Hu, Yuheng, Lydia Manikonda, and Subbarao Kambhampati. "What We Instagram: A First Analysis of Instagram Photo Content and User Types." *International AAAI Conference on Web and Social Media.* 2014.

Instagram. "Instagram." Retrieved April 8, 2016. (http://www.instagram.com).

Kawasaki, Guy. *The Art of Social Media: Power Tips for Power Users.* New York, NY: Penguin Group, 2014.

Perez, Sarah. "Snapchat is now the #3 social app among millennials." TechCrunch, August 11, 2014. (http://www.techcrunch.com/2014/08/11/snapchat-is-now-the-3-social-app-among-millennials).

Pulizzi, Joe. *Epic Content Marketing: How to Tell a Different Story, Break through the Clutter, and Win More Customers by Marketing Less.* New York, NY: McGraw-Hill Education, 2013.

Rusli, Evelyn M., and Douglas MacMillan. "Snapchat spurned $3 billion acquisition offer from Facebook." *Wall Street Journal*, November 13, 2013.

Salomon, Danielle. "Moving on from Facebook: Using Instagram to connect with undergraduates and engage in teaching and learning." *College & Research Libraries News* 74, no. 8 (2013): 408–412.

Snapchat. "Snapchat." Retrieved April 8, 2016. (http://www.snapchat.com).

Stelzner, Michael. "Visual Social Media, How Images Improve Your Social Media Marketing." *Social Media Examiner*, January 31, 2014. (http://www.socialmediaexaminer.com/visual-social-media-with-donna-moritz).

Suber, Howard. *The Power of Film.* Studio City, CA: Michael Wiese Productions, 2006.

Vaynerchuk, Gary. *Jab, Jab, Jab, Right Hook: How to Tell Your Story in a Noisy Social World.* New York, NY: *HarperBusiness*, 2013.

Walter, Ekatarina. "The Rise of Visual Social Media." Fast Company. August 28, 2012. (http://www.fastcompany.com/3000794/rise-visual-social-media).

INDEX

A

Activity, 14

B

Bieber, Justin, 22
bio, 11–13, 27
Burbn, 7
  Systrom, Kevin, 6–7
  Krieger, Mike, 7

C

chief executive officer
  (CEO), 9
comment, 7, 14, 17,

D

direct message (DM), 14

E

Explore, 14

F

Facebook, 7, 10–11, 13,
  17, 26,
filter, 13, 16, 34,

follower, 10–12, 18–19,
  24–25, 28, 32, 36–37, 40,
  44, 47

G

geotag, 15
Google, 7

H

handle, 13–14
hashtag, 10, 14, 16–17, 46,
Hayes, Alex, 10

I

Instagram Direct, 16–17

L

LiveJournal, 6
like, 10, 14, 19, 24

M

metrics, 24–25
Murphy, Bobby, 9

N

Nextstop.com, 7
newsfeed, 11, 29

ABOUT THE AUTHOR

Eduardo Lopez is a strategist at Porter Novelli, a global marketing and communications agency. He focuses on exploring how language and culture shape our behavior. For the past six years, he's worked on digital strategy and content marketing programs for Sony PlayStation, T-Mobile, HP Inc., Capital One, and LinkedIn. Before working in marketing, Lopez was a behavior analyst and spent two years researching persuasion in a social psychology laboratory.

PHOTO CREDITS

Cover Hero Images/Getty Images; p. 3 everything possible/Shutterstock.com; pp. 4–5 background solarseven/Shutterstock.com; pp. 4–5 (inset) Blend Images/Shutterstock.com; p. 7 John Fedele/Blend Images/Getty Images; p. 8 Justin Sullivan/Getty Images; p. 9 J.Emilio Flores/Corbis News/Getty Images; p. 12 IM_VISUALS/Shutterstock.com; p. 15 SpeedKingz/Shutterstock.com; p. 18 © iStockphoto.com/Fly_dragonfly; p. 21 © iStockphoto.com/Tarik Kizilkaya; pp. 24, 25, 38 Rawpixel.com/Shutterstock.com; p. 28 Bloomberg/Getty Images; p. 30 © AP Images; p. 32 Wittybear/Shutterstock.com; p. 36 Lester Cohen/BBMA2016/Getty Images; p. 41 wundervisuals/E+/Getty Images; p. 42 Compassionate Eye Foundation/Chris Windsor/DigitalVision/Getty Images; p. 44 Blend Images – Hill Street Studios/Brand X Pictures/Getty Images; p. 46 Tooga/Taxi/Getty Images; p. 49 Rodrigo Varela/Getty Images; p. 50 Neustockimages/E+/Getty Images; interior pages checklist icon D Line/Shutterstock.com; back cover background photo Rawpixel.com/Shutterstock.com.

Designer: Michael Moy; Photo Researcher: Karen Huang